Safe Handling
a poem

Safe Handling
a poem

by Rebecca Evans

~ 2024 ~

Safe Handling
© Copyright 2024 Rebecca Evans
All rights reserved. No part of this book may be used or reproduced in any manner whatsoever without written permission from either the author or the publisher, except in the case of credited epigraphs or brief quotations embedded in articles or reviews.

Editor-in-chief
Eric Morago

Editor Emeritus
Michael Miller

Marketing Specialist
Ellen Webre

Copy editors
Betty Rodgers
Jeremy Ra

Front cover art
Rebecca Evans

Book design
Michael Wada

Moon Tide logo design
Abraham Gomez

Safe Handling
is published by Moon Tide Press

Moon Tide Press
6709 Washington Ave. #9297
Whittier, CA 90608
www.moontidepress.com

FIRST EDITION

Printed in the United States of America

ISBN # 978-1-957799-18-6

Further Praise For *Safe Handling*

Safe Handling is heart-wrenching and beautiful and dare I say: perfect. A mother's love, her profound love, wrapped in words that will leave you holding your breath. Rebecca Evans has written a magnificent poem about the human heart - her son's heart - and I have no doubt - none - that she will move and open yours.

— Amy Ferris, *Mighty Gorgeous, A Little Book About Messy Love*

Safe Handling takes readers deeply into the experience of a mother treading the line between life and death with her son, a precarious zone "near rupture,/near rapture." This is a brave and moving book-length poem, a poem brimming with potent questions and even more potent love. "Didn't I read Emily and Maya to feel less alone?" asks Rebecca Evans, and I know her work will do the same, will offer solidarity for those who've lived through similar situations, and stoke deep empathy in those who haven't. What lucky readers we are to be held in Evans' safe, skilled, hands.

— Gayle Brandeis, PEN and Bellwether Prize recipient

Safe Handling, a memoir poem about the grace and beauty of the human experience, testifies to the resilience of the human spirit. As Evans witnesses her son undergo another surgery, she unpacks the heart›s delicate contents—fear, innocence, and unwavering love. Through beautiful language and mastery of the craft, Rebecca Evans transforms the personal into a universal story of vulnerability and humanity. *Safe Handling* is a map and a must-read for those who love fiercely and must

— C. Marie Fuhrman, *Camped Beneath the Dam: Poems*

A single obsession, a prayer, a testament. A litany of questions no one wants to ask, no one wants to answer, no one wants to hear. A mother's response to a thousand terrors and a single question from a tiny, reconstructed, child ("Will this hurt as much as my last surgery?") Rebecca Evans' chapbook, is both a cri de couer and a triumph. It is a solitary poem, born in hospitals, bred from love, and brought into the world from a unique and spectacular courage. *Safe Handling* is not only moving - it is an inspirational blueprint for extraordinary mothering, survival, and, in the end, joy.

— Dr Harrison Solow, Pushcart Prize for Literature recipient

Love and worry, relief and desire, heart and hurt, need and responsibility, grief and grace are all folded carefully into the lines and white spaces of *Safe Handling*, by Rebecca Evans. These things a mother carries accumulate in the stanzas and margins of this expansive and beautiful long poem, forming a rich and heartfelt narrative. Read this. It will fill you like a deep and necessary breath.

— Patricia Ann McNair, *The Temple of Air*

Striking similar chords to Edward Hirsch's renowned *Gabriel*, Evans' collection-length poem *Safe Handling* is a deeply moving experience. In these vibrant poems of family and how our identities change with family dynamics, of a journey through our health care system and the heartbreak and hope associated with such a journey, Evans exhibits a true talent for imbuing mundane details with authenticity, layered meanings, and linguistic beauty. But *Safe Handling* is so much more than that; it's also brimming with deep longing, pain, and the kinds of contrasts that speak to larger human truths. Filled with rich and accessible language, these poems are intellectually stimulating and emotionally engaging, written by someone with clear eyes and an open, curious heart.

—John Sibley Williams, *As One Fire Consumes Another*

Under normal usage, "Safe Handling" is how we carry weight or move an object, but in this insightful collection of poems, it becomes the operative metaphor for how we lift the heart, how we hold it carefully, how we pack and unpack it like luggage, and how, when we love children whose health may be compromised, we do so without compromise, but often without the housing of safety. Instead, we create, as best we can and against all odds, a safe grace—even when physical safety is illusory. In beautifully crafted light-filled sections, Rebecca Evans narrates her mother/son story, one that rebuilds a broken world—one where the safe handling of our fears is an act of resilience and reconstruction—both of the body and the mind. Here is mother love in abundance and a boy of great courage.

— Anne-Marie Oomen, *As Long As I Know You: The Mom Book*,

Safe Handling is a gripping, finely crafted journey that pulls us through the intense experience of heart surgery for a child. Laced with courage, pain, kindness, and strength, this poem by Rebecca Evans pulses with a through-line of mother-child-love and touches us deeply. Brilliant and triumphant, it must be read. Again and again.

— Guy Biederman, *Nova Nights*

In Rebecca Evans' new book of poetry titled *Safe Handling*, we witness the faces of fright, death, and the mystery of rescue rendered in tight and spare verse. Urgent, hopeful, compassionate, and courageous words. Herein reside bones and gristle, blood, a mother's fierce drive to protect a child, and we the readers are suspended in a time and place out of our control. We watch, we listen, we feel. Redemptive poetry, resonant with life's essence.

— Ken Rodgers, co-producer, *I Married the War*

for Zach

Safe Handling

Our luggage rests, perched across from us, pre-op
    at Sacred Heart Medical Center, Spokane

My son settles on the bed's edge, ankles crossed
    feet swinging, his grin reaching his ears. He asks

What's for dinner? Did you remember to tell Granny I'm here? Are you glad it's just us? Do you think my brothers miss me? Miss me already? What is your face doing? Is that your thinking face or worried face? It's not an angry face. Do we have to bring our suitcases everywhere

the air between us thin, like a fragile artery near rupture,
    near rapture. I nod. I smile. I stand. I adjust his paper gown

*

Five years before, my son outgrew that hospital crib. I've yet
    to outgrow sterile white, stain-
    less steel, singe of antiseptic and sickness
    and the twisting of my hands, of my heart

Our luggage is a struggle as we—my son and me—
    wait, long-listed for a stay at Ronald McDonald House

My son fidgets, loosens, then accidentally unties
    his gown, the type that helps him look like everyone

Can you fix it? How long before the doctor gets here? Will this hurt as much as my last surgery? The one when they cut open my eye muscles? Or the one before that? Which one was the one before that? Do you remember, Mom? Mom? Are you worried

May, 2013: I'm fulltime studenting and overtime single-
mothering, my amulet—engraved with Birkat Kohanim—
    dangles 'round my neck

*

My son stretches his arm straight
    anxious for the blood pressure cuff
    nods and reminds himself aloud
    It's only a tiny hug for my arm

I tug our luggage to the Medicaid-paid motel, where, out
    front, a man pockets a gun, and another, hides a blade

My son's pacemaker kick-starts, shoots awake when his heart
    stops. It does. Stop. Now it needs new batteries

Am I the only one who grieves his grayness? Sees his heart slow? Oh! how his fragile body de-fibbed itself to life and we—his cardiologist and me— thought he suffered seizures. Remember that pediatric neurologist who said, "Nothing's wrong." And I told him

I wonder the number of things wrong with me, if I need
    new batteries too, should some sort of spark break my heart

                                        *

Two weeks prior, I'd received approvals from American Medical
    Response (AMR) mostly flights and meals for us—
    my son and me until we needed more proof to clear
        security, to avoid airport scanners that damage his device

I drag our luggage, escape that seedy motel to our waiting cab
    unload us—my son and me—into the hospital lobby

My son sleeps on my chest. Even though he's 12, he's little
    larger than toddler-size in body and brain. He snores

What will I say if that nurse asks why we are sleeping in the lobby?
What will I ask of her? What if they ask us to leave? Will that rain ever
stop? Where can I safely keep us—my son and me— until surgery or
until a bed at The House frees? Why are there never enough beds

3 am and we—my son and me and our luggage—settle side by side
    in the lobby. The couch arm tweed frays beneath my fingers

*

This pre-op, the first time we—my son and me—see
    the surgeon, the man who'll scalpel through
    my son's chest cavity. He enters and regards
    our luggage, then us. I cross my arms, hold myself

I pre-packed our luggage days ahead. They said my son's pacer
        could last at least a week, the battery depleted, critically low

He sips apple juice from Styrofoam and asks for more. I pull
        his socks, rub his feet, ask for an extra blanket. I ask

Did I remember: my charger, my mouse, my flash drive, the weather?
Soft socks for us—my son and me—protein bars, that thick file of endless
documents, important numbers, cash? Do I have cash? We—my sons and
me—run out of money. We're always depleted

My two younger sons remain behind, stay with friends, I've no
        family near. I've no help. No. I've family—my sons and me

*

The surgeon shakes our—my son's, then my—
        hands, tells my son, *This is easy-peasy*
        and I like that he talks to my son
        instead of me. Like that he sees my son

I corner our luggage, the room crowded—my son and me,
    the doctor, the nurse, the intern (with permission)

My son tells his surgeon that his heart beats the Scooby-
    Doo song. The surgeon grins, asks if he has questions

Will I feel it when you cut me open? Will I feel the new batteries inside? Will I have ever-ready energy? Will I have more time to play? Will you sign my chest like I have a cast? Yes. I've been casted. Both feet. Not anymore. See? AFOs and they aren't heavy. When will the rain stop

I want to ask if they'll open him through his old incision, scrape
    scar tissue and tendril winding 'round wires. I don't

*

The intern returns to pre-op, says
    the surgeon funded us a room 'cross the way
    It's a five-star, sheets starched and stretched
    I can toss a stone and *clink* the hospital's front door

I unpack our—my son's and my—luggage. Hang soft tees
      and tuck clean underwear in drawers. Someone knocks

We've no peephole to peek and pre-protect us—
      my son and me—here, at this hotel. Two bearded rabbis

*How did I forget Shabbat? How did they know we—my son and me—
are here? They brought challah and hummus and grape juice and, look
at me, eating it all. When was my last meal? How I feel for my son,
fasting for surgery, tempted but not touching this food. Two candles too*

I light candles, one for each of us—my son and me—I circle
      my palms, press light into me, chant a prayer, linger here

*

I remember my prayer book, tattered and over-used
    relied upon in days of flight and famine
  I remember the foodbank lines and the worry
    of empty cupboards and that hunger. Always hunger

Luggage, emptied and stowed in the hotel closet
    I hope to feel settled in, I hope to feel settled, I hope to feel

While my son sleeps, I check his chest for the rise, the fall
    I type through the night, finish a paper or a poem or

Since childhood, didn't books offer escape? My journals provide therapy? Didn't I read Emily and Maya to feel less alone? When I took to coursework, didn't I think I could nudge this little poet trapped inside, nurture her into writing? Didn't I pen my first poem in fourth grade

I type only by computer light, roll challah chunks into bite-
    size doughballs, scoop hummus, swig juice to wash it

*

I pace our—my son's and my—room at 5 am, do push-
    ups with my feet on the edge of the bed. Tricep-
    dip away my excess energy and my worry and my
    challah. I wake my son at the last possible minute

I leave our luggage at the hotel the next morning. We—
    my son and me—arrive at 7. Still in my same shirt and jeans

Bagless and in the lobby, my teeth unbrushed, my hair uncombed
    my son already under. I tug the couch's loose threads

What if his heart stops during surgery? What if the scalpel slips? More things go wrong than right. This is what, his 33rd procedure? Who told me, "Every time you go under the knife you die a little?" Don't we die a little all the time? How many beats does he have left? How many do I

You cannot know how long you've held your breath, paused your beat
    when you've a child with node and valve dysfunction, when
    you've a child

*

The lobby swarms this fine surgical morning, mostly with TV
    Chatter, the station tuned to a flip-your-home show
    the nurses whisper to no one in particular as supply
    carts whistle by, wheels wobbly, uneven, worn

I often feel like luggage—not the pretty matching set—more akin
    to hand-me-down second-hand baggage, used and empty

The surgeon approaches, snaps off his gloves
    His worn expression, worn. He clears his throat

Is my son still here? Success? Why is the rain so loud? A simple battery change. How many times have I swapped a dud—from remote, vibrator, Walkman—this mindless act of energy exchange? When did I start storing batteries in the fridge? Who told me cold could maintain longevity

My spine stretches. I nod. I pull curls tangling my lashes,
    everything damp—sweat or tears—who can say

*

Medical personnel are trained to remain emotionally disconnected.
    They can't perform if they care too much.
    Or at all. They keep clean and clear
        steel slates. This surgeon funds our—my son's and my—stay

Thank you for the room, I say, and, *It's nice to not have to trek our
        luggage 'round.* The surgeon nods, stays standing

I watch my feet tap air, bite my lip, my tongue, my fist. He
        touches my arm, says, *Go see him,* and, *He's in recovery*

*Recovery? He's already healing? Will you look at him—my son—go?
Do you see the way he keeps going? How his heart persists. Is that my
heart pounding out a beat? Some familiar song? What is it? It can't be
Garbage or Depeche Mode. Could it be "Dry the Rain"*

I stand before he—the surgeon—finishes
        I'm waving to the nurse's station. I'm happy. I'm waving

*

They encase recovery rooms in glass
        I wonder if this is for the patient, the family or the doctor.
        Moans and beeps and hums ring from every room,
        all in time with earth-song, all in time

How little we—my son and me—need to carry. Without our luggage
    there's only me and my feet and my ID and my iPhone

And how much I carried when my womb stretched and shaped
    'round him, like a girdle, a bandage, a garment bag

Do you wonder why I'm alone when my belly once filled with son after son? Wonder how I filled with their father as well? Wonder if he, their father, is unwell? Does it matter—well or unwell—if his heart works wrong and he is incapable of providing? Incapable of offering a safe place

Maybe the only reason the hotel across from the hospital
    seems safer than the flea-sirened motel is measure, proximity

*

Three years before this, I fled my now-ex-and-unsafe husband,
    and we—my three sons and me—hid in a safe house. I
    never knew such a thing existed. A house holding safety
    For six weeks we laid low. We didn't move. We didn't blink

Post-op and lazing in the hotel, we—my son and me and our unpacked
    luggage—until his face balloons blowfish-like

I do not wait. I do not hesitate. I call a cab. The hospital
    a stone's throw, remember? I auto-pilot into gathering

Do you think I move mindlessly? Do I gather my son, myself, his favorite blanket, our toothbrushes? Do I load us into the cab, tell the driver, "ER?" Does my body react without my mind? Does the driver nod as he steers? Before the cab stops, am I out

Wheelchairs parked in rows—like soldiers—at the Emergency
    entrance. The staff hustles noting my haste

*

ER's manage emergencies based on severity, on triage—a
    concept conceived in 17th century Egypt—dividing injured
    into categories, like kingdoms of living things. Later, they
    prioritized soldiers. I tell the doctors, *My son's a soldier*

This luggage-less space, the nonclinical, nontrainable aspect of medicine
reminds me to remind myself, *It's a practice, not a science*

My son, red-faced and face-up on the table, fevered as he endures
an *event*—their label—like a wedding, a soccer game, a graduation

*Ohmylordohmylord. Have they forgotten I'm here? Am I roaming in some
foreign country—Occlusion, Obstruction, Orifice? How do I not know this
language? Why can't I see over anyone? How does this room fill so quickly?
And in raindrop beats, they leave. There...there*

There, there, I say to my sons whenever they hurt, and now
I say this to myself. His chest—it rises, it falls, it keeps going

*

They tell me, *Staph infection*. Tell me, *IV antibiotics*. Tell
me, *Relax*, and *He's fine*. I know this word, *Fine*
and the way we pretend and respond and weaponize
truth with this single syllable. I tell myself, I am

Baggage. Who decided our hurt is baggage? Why not name
    our pain *luggage*—something we can unpack

The nurse gazes across the operating table, locks my eyes
    her lashes wet and wilty. She is not sterile like the others

Do you know my heart is more defective than my son's? Know I'm more disabled than most? Know some call this, "Hidden?" Do you know me? Do I even know myself? Do you know that I'm slow to sleep and quick to anxiety and that there are few open spaces between

I realize I rarely cry. I might have few tears remaining.
    Maybe I've worn out my heart, too. Maybe worn away

*

Now we wait. The most difficult times in life
    require extended periods of waiting
        War. Dying. Silence. How the human heart
    endures long, lone hours, months, years

We—my son and me—ambulance back to our luggage and hotel
    I curl my body 'round him like a shell, a cocoon, a petal

We—my son and me—ride back and forth, back and forth three more days.
    They clear him for flight, as if he were a plane

Doesn't he hate the dressing and re-dressing in this gown? The snipping and unsnipping of the wristband that holds his name, his birthday? What's the difference between a hospital institution and a military machine? Don't we all dress the same, tagged with rank, name, serial number

By now, I've forgotten to write my poems, my papers I've forgotten
    I'm a student or a person. I'm a sentinel, a warrior, a

*

We load first with the other fragile passengers
    my son takes to a window seat and I harness
    him in with a small pillow padding his chest, protecting
    stitches. Six inches long—this scar extends past
    the one before. One on top of one on top of one another

My carry-on carries my son's equipment, the machine that measures
    his heart-pace. Someone helps me, helps stow the bag overhead

Our flight, brief, and our home-greeting, teary with nervous laughter
    Oh! how his brothers worry and how little I can offer

Should we cuddle, all four of us? Build a blanket fort? Watch movies until we doze? Should I pop popcorn drizzled with real butter? And tomorrow, do you think we should pack a picnic? One for breakfast? Load dessert for dinner? Should we do this every day? Should we do this

By nightfall, they—my three sons—curve like nesting Russian
    dolls, one alongside the other, alongside the other

                            *

I sit watch watching their rises, their falls. I'm sure they
    pace a rhythm, one lulling the other in harmony. I stay
    this way 'til sun breaks free of Idaho's mountain line—
    and here, I pause. Here, I silently cry as magenta and ochre
    burst open and free this rainless sky

Acknowledgements

To my three sons, who lifted me, carried me, gave me purpose, I am forever indebted. Thank you, Zachary (Raphael), Preston (Michael), and Julian (Yehudah). To the unnamed surgeon at Sacred Heart Medical Center, who gifted us—Zach and me—not only a room but hope and a reminder that kindness alleviates suffering. To the poetic influence of Edward Hirsch and his beautiful book-length poem, *Gabriel*, which became the inspiration for this body of work. Thanks to Brian Turner for friendship, mentorship, and introducing me to Hirsch's work. To Gayle Brandeis for her continuous love, encouragement, and incredible editorial skills. To Betty Rodgers for her generosity, love, and keen copy edits. To Ken Rodgers for keeping me on a poetic course no matter. And to Moon Tide Press for supporting this and earlier projects, helping my words find their way into the world.

About the Author

Rebecca Evans writes the difficult, the heart-full, the guidebooks for survivors. Her debut memoir in verse, *Tangled by Blood*, bridges motherhood and betrayal, untangling wounds and re-storying what it means to be a mother. She's a memoirist, essayist, and poet, infusing her love of empowerment with craft. She teaches high school teens in the Juvie system through journaling and art projects. Rebecca is also a military veteran, a practicing Jew, a self-taught gardener, and shares space with four Newfoundlands and her sons. She specializes in writing workshops for those diving deep into narrative. She co-hosts Radio Boise's Writer to Writer show on Stray theater and does her best writing in a hidden cove beneath her stairway.

She's earned two MFAs, one in creative nonfiction, the other in poetry, University of Nevada, Reno at Lake Tahoe. Her poems and essays have appeared in *Narratively, Brevity, The Rumpus, Hypertext Magazine, War, Literature and the Arts, The Limberlost Review,* and more, along with a handful of anthologies.

She's co-edited an anthology of poems, *When There Are Nine*, a tribute to the life and achievements of Ruth Bader Ginsburg (Moon Tide Press, 2022). Her full-length poetry collection, a memoir-in-verse, *Tangled by Blood* (Moon Tide Press. 2023), is available wherever fine books are sold. Visit her at www.rebeccaevanswriter.com.

Also Available from Moon Tide Press

More Jerkumstances: New & Selected Poems, Barbara Eknoian (2024)
Dissection Day, Ally McGregor (2023)
He's a Color Until He's Not, Christian Hanz Lozada (2023)
The Language of Fractions, Nicelle Davis (2023)
Paradise Anonymous, Oriana Ivy (2023)
Now You Are a Missing Person, Susan Hayden (2023)
Maze Mouth, Brian Sonia-Wallace (2023)
Tangled by Blood, Rebecca Evans (2023)
Another Way of Loving Death, Jeremy Ra (2023)
Kissing the Wound, J.D. Isip (2023)
Feed It to the River, Terhi K. Cherry (2022)
*Beat Not Beat: An Anthology of California Poets Screwing
    on the Beat and Post-Beat Tradition* (2022)
*When There Are Nine: Poems Celebrating the Life and Achievements
    of Ruth Bader Ginsburg* (2022)
The Knife Thrower's Daughter, Terri Niccum (2022)
2 Revere Place, Aruni Wijesinghe (2022)
Here Go the Knives, Kelsey Bryan-Zwick (2022)
Trumpets in the Sky, Jerry Garcia (2022)
Threnody, Donna Hilbert (2022)
A Burning Lake of Paper Suns, Ellen Webre (2021)
Instructions for an Animal Body, Kelly Gray (2021)
Head *V* Heart: New & Selected Poems, Rob Sturma (2021)
*Sh!t Men Say to Me: A Poetry Anthology in Response
    to Toxic Masculinity* (2021)
Flower Grand First, Gustavo Hernandez (2021)
Everything is Radiant Between the Hates, Rich Ferguson (2020)
When the Pain Starts: Poetry as Sequential Art, Alan Passman (2020)
This Place Could Be Haunted If I Didn't Believe in Love,
    Lincoln McElwee (2020)
Impossible Thirst, Kathryn de Lancellotti (2020)
Lullabies for End Times, Jennifer Bradpiece (2020)
Crabgrass World, Robin Axworthy (2020)
Contortionist Tongue, Dania Ayah Alkhouli (2020)

The only thing that makes sense is to grow, Scott Ferry (2020)
Dead Letter Box, Terri Niccum (2019)
Tea and Subtitles: Selected Poems 1999-2019, Michael Miller (2019)
At the Table of the Unknown, Alexandra Umlas (2019)
The Book of Rabbits, Vince Trimboli (2019)
Everything I Write Is a Love Song to the World,
    David McIntire (2019)
Letters to the Leader, HanaLena Fennel (2019)
Darwin's Garden, Lee Rossi (2019)
Dark Ink: A Poetry Anthology Inspired by Horror (2018)
Drop and Dazzle, Peggy Dobreer (2018)
Junkie Wife, Alexis Rhone Fancher (2018)
The Moon, My Lover, My Mother, & the Dog,
    Daniel McGinn (2018)
Lullaby of Teeth: An Anthology of Southern California Poetry (2017)
Angels in Seven, Michael Miller (2016)
A Likely Story, Robbi Nester (2014)
Embers on the Stairs, Ruth Bavetta (2014)
The Green of Sunset, John Brantingham (2013)
The Savagery of Bone, Timothy Matthew Perez (2013)
The Silence of Doorways, Sharon Venezio (2013)
Cosmos: An Anthology of Southern California Poetry (2012)
Straws and Shadows, Irena Praitis (2012)
In the Lake of Your Bones, Peggy Dobreer (2012)
I Was Building Up to Something, Susan Davis (2011)
Hopeless Cases, Michael Kramer (2011)
One World, Gail Newman (2011)
What We Ache For, Eric Morago (2010)
Now and Then, Lee Mallory (2009)
Pop Art: An Anthology of Southern California Poetry (2009)
In the Heaven of Never Before, Carine Topal (2008)
A Wild Region, Kate Buckley (2008)
Carving in Bone: An Anthology of Orange County Poetry (2007)
Kindness from a Dark God, Ben Trigg (2007)
A Thin Strand of Lights, Ricki Mandeville (2006)
Sleepyhead Assassins, Mindy Nettifee (2006)
Tide Pools: An Anthology of Orange County Poetry (2006)
Lost American Nights: Lyrics & Poems, Michael Ubaldini (2006)

Patrons

Moon Tide Press would like to thank the following people for their support in helping publish the finest poetry from the Southern California region. To sign up as a patron, visit www.moontidepress.com or send an email to publisher@moontidepress.com.

Anonymous
Robin Axworthy
Conner Brenner
Nicole Connolly
Bill Cushing
Susan Davis
Kristen Baum DeBeasi
Peggy Dobreer
Kate Gale
Dennis Gowans
Alexis Rhone Fancher
HanaLena Fennel
Half Off Books &
Brad T. Cox
Donna Hilbert
Jim & Vicky Hoggatt
Michael Kramer
Ron Koertge &
Bianca Richards
Gary Jacobelly
Ray & Christi Lacoste
Jeffery Lewis
Zachary &
Tammy Locklin
Lincoln McElwee

David McIntire
José Enrique Medina
Michael Miller &
Rachanee Srisavasdi
Michelle & Robert Miller
Ronny & Richard Morago
Terri Niccum
Andrew November
Jeremy Ra
Luke &
Mia Salazar
Jennifer Smith
Roger Sponder
Andrew Turner
Rex Wilder
Mariano Zaro
Wes Bryan Zwick